MW01097723

Vintage

Blossoms and Birds

A Grayscale Adult Coloring Book

48 Vintage Coloring Pages

Grayscale Coloring Books

VOLUME 57

Vicki Becker

About the Author

Vicki Becker is an avid needlework enthusiast who loves everything arts and crafts! Mrs. Becker has been knitting and crocheting for over 48 years. She learned to crochet from her grandmother in the beautiful Adirondack Mountains of upstate New York where she grew up.

Mrs. Becker shares her knowledge and experience through her books with patterns for crochet, knitting, hand embroidery, and quilting. Vicki also enjoys making puzzle books, journals, and coloring books. She creates digital art, illustrations, and mixed media art for the designs in her books.

Vicki Becker lives in central Florida with her husband, four cats, and two dogs. Her hobbies include all forms of needlework, photography, digital art, cooking, and gardening.

What Is Grayscale Coloring?

Grayscale coloring means that you will be coloring over a black-and-white picture. The magic of coloring over grayscale is that the shading is already done for you! Even beginners with no knowledge of shading can achieve beautiful results. Colored pencils work beautifully with the grayscale images giving the finished picture depth and dimension. The paper is well suited for colored pencils but does not work as well with markers. If you use markers put a sheet of paper under the page in case of bleed-through.

ISBN-13: 978-1979933025

ISBN-10: 1979933022

First Printing, 2017
Printed in the United States of America

Colorists Name

Date

Colorists Name

Date

Colorists Name

Date

Colorists Name

Date

Colorists Name

Date

Colorists Name

Date

Colorists Name

Date

Colorists Name

Date

Colorists Name

Date

Colorists Name

Date

Colorists Name

Date

Colorists Name

Date

Colorists Name

Date

Colorists Name

Date

Colorists Name

Date

Colorists Name

Date

Colorists Name

Date

Colorists Name

Date

Colorists Name

Date

Colorists Name

Date

Colorists Name

Date

Colorists Name

Date

Colorists Name

Date

Colorists Name

Date

Colorists Name

Date

Colorists Name

Date

Colorists Name

Date

Colorists Name

Date

Colorists Name

Date

Colorists Name

Date

Colorists Name

Date

Colorists Name

Date

Colorists Name

Date

Colorists Name

Date

Colorists Name

Date

Colorists Name

Date

Colorists Name

Date

Colorists Name

Date

Colorists Name

Date

Colorists Name

Date

Colorists Name

Date

Colorists Name

Date

Colorists Name

Date

Colorists Name

Date

Colorists Name

Date

Colorists Name

Date

Colorists Name

Date

Made in United States
North Haven, CT
20 March 2022

17359373R00057